My
GERMAN
Ancestor

A **Zap** The Grandma Gap Activity Book

By Janet Hovorka & Amy Slade

How To Use This Book

This activity book is designed to help create stronger bonds in modern families by encouraging the whole family to learn about their ancestors together. Greater knowledge about family history especially strengthens and empowers youth by creating self-esteem, resilience and a greater sense of control over their lives. Studying the family's past also strengthens the relationships between living family members by creating a shared experience and core identity that no one else in the world can duplicate. Young people can take the lead to accomplish the activities in this book with their family members.

It is our hope that learning about your family's past together can be a fun and exciting adventure and that this book will help all of your family members discover joy in the quest to find out more about your ancestors.

Janet Hovorka   *Amy Slade*

Illustrated by Bob Bonham http://www.coroflot.com/bbonham

While the authors have made every effort to provide accurate internet addresses at the time of publication, neither the authors nor the publisher assume any responsibility for changes that occur after publication. Further, neither the author nor publisher assume any responsibility for third party websites or their contents.

Published by Family ChartMasters
P.O. Box 1080 Pleasant Grove, Utah 84062
www.familychartmasters.com 801-872-4278
For more information, free downloads, quantity discounts and new resources go to
www.zapthegrandmagap.com

International Standard Book Number: 978-09888-548-5-7

Table of Contents

Introduction

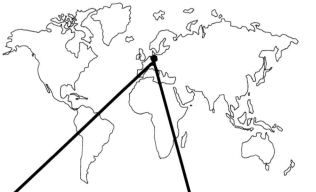

If you have German ancestors, you are really lucky. Germany is a beautiful country in the center of Europe. Germany has made a major political, religious and cultural impact on the world with many important philosphers, inventors, musicians, scholars and scientists. The history of Germany as united country is relatively short. It was formed from many small states ruled by dukes and kings who united in 1871. However the German people had previously shared the same language, culture and traditions for thousands of years.

If you have one German ancestor, you probably have several German ancestors. For this book, you may want to focus on the one you know the most about or the one most interesting to you, but feel free to add other pages in the back of the book with more information about other ancestors.

Sections of this Book

The workbook starts with pages to fill in what you know about your ancestors and instructions on where to look for more information. Then there are pages with common cultural experiences which work like puzzle pieces to help fill in what the day to day lives of your ancestors were like. The pages with references that are not specific to your family members are marked at the bottom of the page with puzzle pieces. While you may not be sure that your ancestors experienced all of the details of this cultural knowledge, these are common experiences shared by many German people in the past and they very likely apply to your family.

How Am I Related To My German Ancestors?

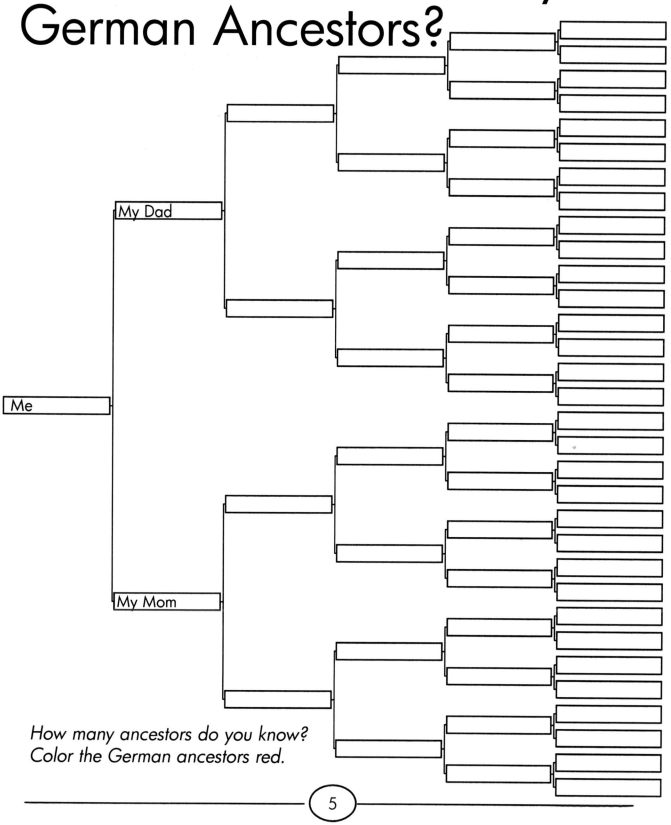

Me

My Dad

My Mom

How many ancestors do you know?
Color the German ancestors red.

Where Can I Find More?

Look for clues about your family history around your home.

Where does your family keep their family history pictures and documents?

_____

_____

Who do you need to ask to see them?

_____

_____

Which family members can you ask about your German ancestors?

_____

You could ask them:

- ☐ What do you know about our German ancestors?
- ☐ How am I related to them?
- ☐ Do you know what they looked like? Do you have any pictures?
- ☐ Do you know what their personalities were like?
- ☐ Do you have any family history keepsakes or documents? Who does?
- ☐ How did our family come to live where we live now?
- ☐ What are some stories about my German ancestors?
- ☐ Do you know the origin of our German surname?
- ☐ Are there any recipes, talents, traditions or common sayings that come from our German family history?

Check the questions you want to ask, then arrange a time to ask the questions in a family history interview.

My Ancestor's Childhood

German Ancestor's name _____

He/She was born on _____(date)
in_____(place)

His/Her parents were:

Mother's Name_____   Father's Name_____
Born _____(date)   Born _____(date)
_____(place)   _____(place)
Died _____(date)   Died _____(date)
_____(place)   _____(place)

His/her parents were married _____(date)
_____(place)

His/Her brothers and sisters were:

_____   _____

_____   _____

_____   _____

_____   _____

_____   _____

Where Can I Find Even More?

Don't fret if you don't know everything yet. Just keep looking and learning.

meta.genealogy.net
   German genealogy website that searches 12 different databases
gov.genealogy.net/search/index
   Gazetter to help identify ancestral locations and their jurisdictions
meta.genealogy.net and familysearch.org/learn/wiki/en/Germany
   Two wiki sites with information about how to research your German roots.
familysearch.org
   Huge collection of German church records and other miscellaneous records
ieg-maps.uni-mainz.de
   Historical maps of Germany and Europe
ortsfamilienbuecher.de
   Collection of village heritage books which list vital records for a town
ancestry.com
   Hamburg, Wuerttemberg, Brandenburg and Baden emigration records
christoph.stoepel.net/geogen/en
   German surname distribution map

Translate German websites using translate.google.com or a Google Chrome browser. More German history and culture resources are on page 52.

Early Germans who came to America were sometimes called Palatines or Hessians

My Ancestor's Adult Life

German Ancestor's Spouse's name _____

He/She was born on _____(date)
in_____(place)

They were married _____(date)
_____(place)

These ancestors are my (*circle the right number of "greats"*)
great great great great great great great great great great grandparents.

Their children were:

_____   _____

_____   _____

_____   _____

_____   _____

They lived:

_____   _____

_____   _____

_____   _____

_____   _____

Me and My Ancestor

You are an important descendant of your German Ancestor.

Glue or draw a picture of yourself here.

Your Name_____

Some of your special qualities are:

_____

_____

_____

_____

You inherited some of your characteristics from your ancestors.

Draw or glue a copy of a picture of your ancestor here.

Your Ancestor's Name_____

Some qualities that you share in common:

_____
_____
_____
_____

My Ancestor's Timeline

Fill in the boxes for the times that your ancestor lived.

☐ 1517 Martin Luther wrote the Nintey-five Theses and started the Reformation.

☐ 1555 The Peace of Augsburg gave the rulers of each German state the right to decide the religion of their subjects.

☐ 1618 The Thirty Years War began.

☐ 1685-1750 Johann Sebastian Bach and 1720-1827 Ludwig van Beethoven wrote and performed many musical works.

☐ 1806 The Holy Roman Empire ended when it was defeated by Napoleon.

☐ 1815 The German Confederation was founded to unify the economies of 39 independent German speaking states.

☐ 1871 German states united into one country with a Chancellor.

☐ 1914 Germany joined World War I on the side of Austria.
1919 Germany was defeated and the Treaty of Versailles signed.

☐ 1939 Germany attacked Poland and World War II began.
1945 Hitler commited suicide and Germany surrendered.

☐ 1961 The East German government built the Berlin Wall to keep its citizens from leaving.

☐ 1989-1990 The East German government opened the Berlin Wall and modern Germany was reunited.

Do You Know German?

Complete the puzzle to learn some words your German ancestors used.

German sometimes uses diacritical marks with letters such as:
ä (which usually makes the sound eh as in ted)
ö (which usually makes the sound i as in girl)
ü (which usually makes the sound oo like in mood)
ß (which usually makes the sound ss)
Some of these letters may be found in this puzzle.

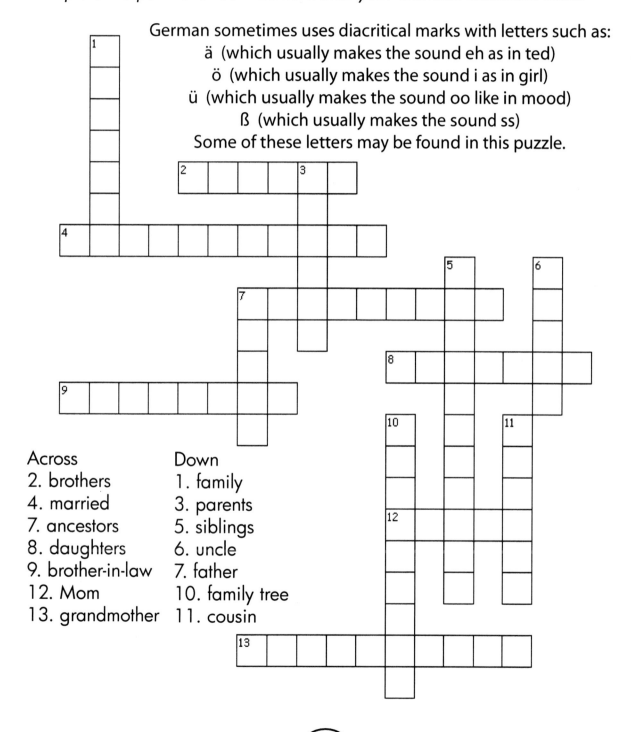

Across
2. brothers
4. married
7. ancestors
8. daughters
9. brother-in-law
12. Mom
13. grandmother

Down
1. family
3. parents
5. siblings
6. uncle
7. father
10. family tree
11. cousin

My Ancestor's Home

Label and draw a red star near where your ancestor lived.

Germany is in the center of
the European continent.
and borders nine countries.

Label these rivers:
Danube, Rhine,
Main, Elbe,
Weser

Label these
forests:
Black Forest,
Bavarian
Forest

Fill in the blanks for
these cities:
Cologne, Düsseldorf,
Stuttgart, Berlin,
Frankfurt, Hannover,
Hamburg, Munich,
Bremen

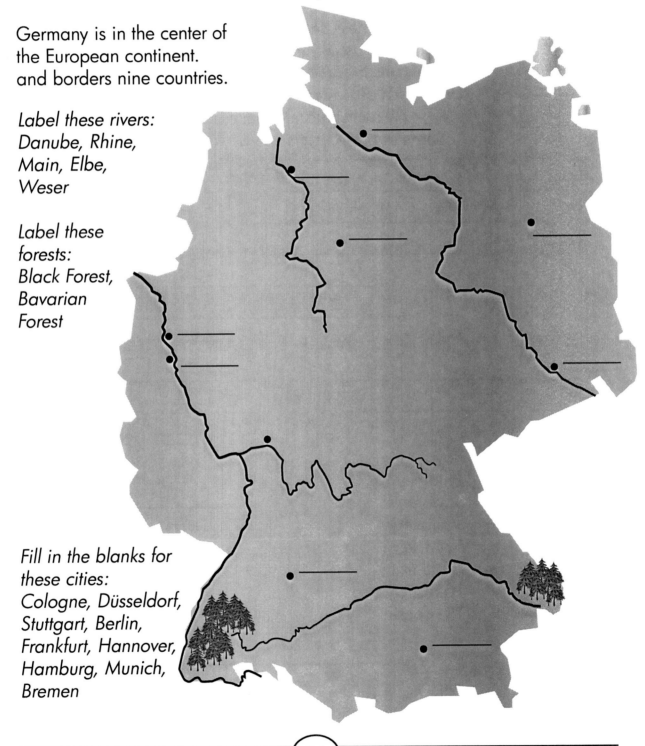

My Ancestor's Journeys

Rivers have always been an important mode of transportation in Germany. German Rivers are easy to navigate and cities were built along the rivers because they were good places for trade. Help your ancestor find their way down the river to the city.

German Länder

German borders have changed many times during many wars. Throughout much of history, small Germanic Länder (states) were ruled by dynasties (families) of princes, dukes, and kings. If your ancestor lived in the German Empire (1871-1918), their hometown may now be in Belgium, Czech Republic, Denmark, France, Lithuania, Poland or Russia

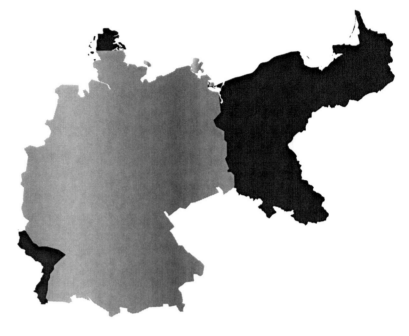

The first chancellor of Germany was a Prussian diplomat who wanted to create a unified German nation. He was the leader of the largest and most powerful state, Brandenburg-Prussia. For many years, he led his state into wars with neighboring states to bring them into one federation. Separate Germanic states unified in 1871 to make the German Empire.

Unscramble the names of some of the historic kingdoms in the German Empire (1871-1918) and solve the puzzle to find the name of Germany's first Chancellor.

LEIPP

LEKCBU
    4   10

SIARUPS
  8   5 7

LUBRONGED
 1

WEIRUNSAHBCG
    3   9

SACLAE RRALNIEO
    6   2

T T   V   M
1   2   2 3   4 5 6   7 8 9 10

Today, each modern German state is derived from a historic state. Germans continue to have a strong tradition of local self government and each modern state has strong administrative and fiscal power.

Find the sixteen states that make up modern Germany in the wordsearch. Circle the area where your ancestors lived in red.

Bavaria	Schleswig-Holstein	Saxony	North Rhine-Westphalia
Bremen	Lower Saxony	Hamburg	Mecklenburg-West Pomerania
Berlin	Saxony-Anhalt	Thuringia	Rhineland-Palatinate
Hesse	Brandenburg	Saarland	Baden-Württemberg

```
N  J  B  K  V  G  E  M  H  B  D  U  I  S  H  I  X  A  A  G
A  I  R  A  V  A  B  E  G  O  R  I  A  N  E  S  X  I  R  N
G  U  D  F  Z  J  Y  C  E  B  W  A  O  G  S  A  G  E  O  N
Z  R  V  O  F  R  D  K  T  P  R  E  N  U  S  G  B  R  D  I
N  G  U  N  M  B  B  L  D  L  F  O  R  D  E  M  T  O  T  E
Y  X  J  B  X  A  K  E  A  A  B  U  O  C  E  H  H  V  N  T
L  Ü  E  G  M  B  M  N  U  T  B  N  Z  T  R  N  J  Q  E  S
N  D  A  W  P  A  D  B  T  T  B  D  T  H  Y  U  B  Q  M  L
B  E  R  L  I  N  H  U  N  S  V  R  I  N  V  J  Z  U  E  O
T  P  T  Y  K  A  Q  R  D  R  Ü  N  O  C  G  C  P  G  R  H
H  B  D  K  B  F  D  G  Z  W  E  X  W  L  Ü  O  B  L  B  G
U  I  P  G  D  O  Z  W  N  W  A  Y  W  C  H  I  Y  S  Q  I
R  I  G  Z  H  A  N  E  E  S  N  B  C  K  U  O  T  C  X  W
I  W  V  Z  F  M  D  S  A  X  O  N  Y  A  N  H  A  L  T  S
N  A  Ü  B  H  A  T  T  M  T  I  F  S  E  R  Q  R  F  F  E
G  H  X  V  B  P  P  P  R  J  C  F  B  B  S  K  K  G  T  L
I  P  C  S  H  T  T  O  H  I  W  A  Z  W  K  Y  Y  G  S  H
A  D  M  A  P  Z  J  M  O  B  Ü  U  H  M  H  E  J  N  I  C
W  H  L  B  D  O  E  E  Q  T  P  J  L  Q  K  X  F  F  D  S
P  I  T  B  S  B  I  R  A  Y  Z  P  Y  C  D  T  F  M  Ü  R
A  E  T  A  N  I  T  A  L  A  P  D  N  A  L  E  N  I  H  R
X  K  H  Q  Z  M  D  N  B  Y  A  Ü  T  I  R  L  A  B  M  J
H  J  C  A  D  Q  C  I  X  D  Y  U  K  F  C  D  W  K  C  A
C  L  H  Y  N  O  X  A  S  R  E  W  O  L  E  I  R  C  T  L
```

German Landmarks

The Brandenburg Gate has been a powerful symbol of Germany throughout its history. It was completed in 1793 and was the main gate to the city of Berlin. If your ancestor ever went to Berlin, they saw the Brandenburg Gate. It was the entry to a boulevard of linden trees which led to the city palace of the Prussian royalty. At the top of the gate is a statue of a goddess with four horses pulling her chariot. The gate was the site of many major historical events.

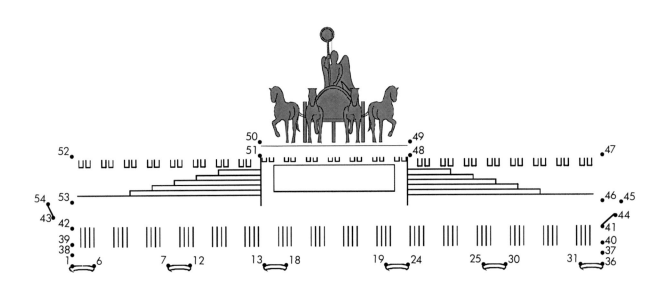

Kings, princes, emperors and dukes built many castles in Germany. Solve this dot to dot puzzle to see Neuschwanstein castle, one of Germany's most recognizable landmarks. Built by "Mad" King Ludwig II in the late 1800s, his builders worked on the castle for 17 years. He spent so much of his own money his people thought he was crazy. Ludwig II only lived in Neuschwanstein castle for 172 days. After he died in 1886 the castle was opened to visitors.

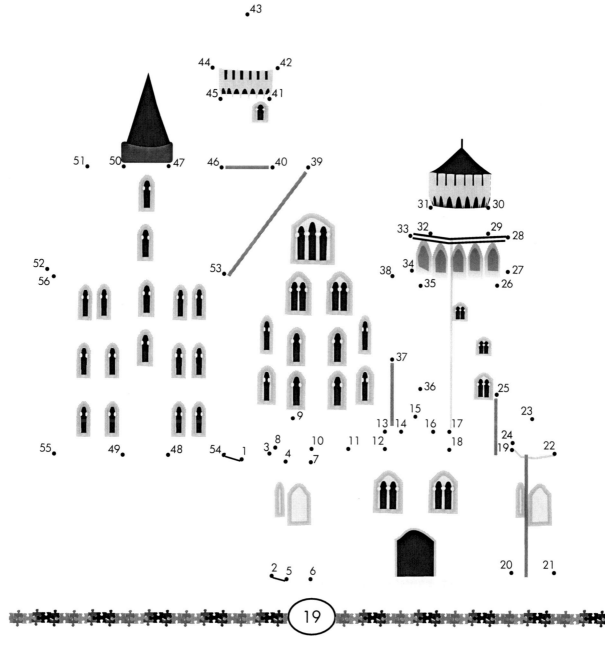

German Innovators

Germans have made many innovations that changed the world of our ancestors. Until the early 1400s every book had to be copied by hand. But around 1440, Johannes Gutenberg invented the printing press which could print dozens of pages a day. The most important book Gutenberg printed was the Bible. For the first time, many people could read the Bible themselves instead of just listening to Bible stories in church.

Gutenberg's Bible made it possible for another German innovator to spark a religious reformation and start a new religion. In 1517 Martin Luther, a German priest, nailed a list of 95 scholarly challenges called "theses" to the door of the church. Many people agreed with him and eventually the new Lutheran church was formed. Other Protestant churches were also formed as people protested against the dominant church.

Gutenberg's press used movable type—letters that could be re-arranged to make different pages and different books. The letters from Gutenberg's press have fallen on the floor. Can you help him put each letter back in the proper place so that he can print the Gutenberg Bible?

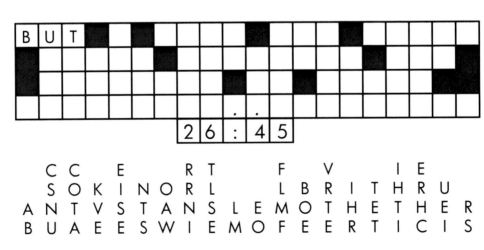

Schultüte School Bag

A Schultüte (also known as a Zuckertuete) is a special gift that German children have received on the first day of school since the early 1800s. They are given to teach children how important education is and to make their first day of school a little sweeter. The Schultüte is a gift from a child's grandparents and parents so that they can feel special on this important day. A Schultüte may be as large a three feet tall. It is decorated and filled with treats such as books, pens, pencils, toys and candy.

Education has always been important to the German people. Germany was the first country in the world to have free public education and "Kindergarten" (or in German, "children's garden") was invented in Germany to prepare children for education by learning through playing together.

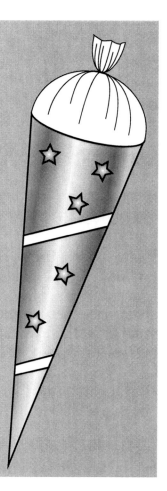

Make your own Schultüte:

- *Cut a large piece of poster board into a square.*
- *Draw pictures and glue glitter, lace, sequins or ribbon on the posterboard.*
- *Take the bottom left corner and roll it up towards the top right corner into a cone shape. Have someone hold your cone while you tape the edges together with strong tape.*
- *Line the cone with tissue paper and leave some sticking out of the top.*
- *Fill the cone with treats, pencils, erasers and small toys.*
- *Use ribbon to tie the tissue paper closed at the top.*

Children of any age can enjoy a Schultüte. Make one for your brother or sister or any member of your family to wish them a successful school year.

A Brüder Grimm Folk Tale

In 1812 two brothers collected and wrote down many of the old German folktales that are now heard all over the world. Jacob (1785 -1863) and Wilhelm (1786-1859) became known as the Brothers Grimm and their stories are known as Grimm's Fairy Tales. "The Pied Piper of Hamelin," "Rumplestiltskin," "Little Red Riding Hood" and "Hansel and Gretel" are a few of their stories.

This is another German folktale retold by the Brothers Grimm. Your ancestor may have heard this story from their parents, who most likely heard it from their parents.

The Goose Girl At The Well

Once upon a time there was an old woman who lived with a flock of geese in a small hut surrounded by forest. Every morning she would hobble out to the forest and collect all the wild fruit she could find and carry everything home on her back. The weight should have been impossible for her to carry, and yet she always managed to bring a full bag home.

One morning a young gentleman came upon the old woman gathering in the forest. "Dear woman," he said, "You cannot carry all of that back to your home."

"Will you help me?" she asked, "You are young and strong and it would only be a small load for you. Besides, my home is not far."

The young man agreed and the old woman placed the bag on his back and two baskets on his arms. "It is quite light," she said.

"No," answered the young gentleman, "it is not light. The weighs as if it is full of cobble-stone or lead. I can scarcely breathe." He wanted to put everything down again, but the old woman would not let him.

"The young gentleman will not carry what I, an old woman, have carried day after day?" She pushed him forward.

They walked on level ground and it was bearable, but when it came to a hill, the young man felt it was beyond his strength. He requested to stop, and even tried to twist and take the

bag of fruit off of his back but it would not move from his back.

"Carry your bundle patiently and I will give you a good gift when we arrive," said the old woman.

And so he continued to crawl along patiently behind the woman. As they continued, the old woman nimbly jumped onto the young gentleman's back as well. When he did not continue walking, the old woman would hit him on the legs with a switch. At long last they reached the old woman's house.

The geese were waiting for the old woman, as was an ugly girl. The girl approached the old woman, "Dear mother, what has happened to make you stay away so long?"

"Nothing has happened. But this nice gentleman offered to take my load, and even carried me when I grew tired." The old woman finally slid off of his back and took the baskets and bundle from him. She looked at him kindly. "You have earned your wages. Take a seat on the bench and I will bring it to you."

"Come daughter," the old woman called, "It is not appropriate for you to be alone with this young man. He may fall in love with you." The old woman and her daughter then went inside of their hut.

The gentleman reclined on the bench under an apple tree, so exhausted that he fell asleep. He only awoke when the old woman shook his shoulder to wake him. She handed him a small box made of emerald. He thanked her and left, glancing back at the hut, the geese, and the daughter.

The gentleman continued traveling until he came upon a large town. Since he knew no one, he was led to the royal palace to meet the King and Queen. He greeted them and gave the queen his little emerald box. The Queen gasped when she opened the box. A pearl lay inside. "How have you come by this pearl?" she asked. The young man answered that he had met an old woman in the woods and had carried a heavy load for her in exchange for the box and pearl. The Queen then began to explain her astonishment.

"We have three daughters. The youngest was kindest and most beautiful of all three. Her skin was fair and her hair as radiant as sunbeams. When she cried, her tears were pearls and jewels.

When she was fifteen, the King summoned all three before him, wanting to determine who of his daughters would inherit his possessions. Whoever loved him the most would get the greater portion. Our first daughter said she loved him more than the sweetest sugar. Our second as much as her prettiest dress. Our youngest daughter replied that she loved her father as much as food loves salt. When the King heard that he was angry. 'If you love me like salt, then that is all you shall get!' he cried. He gave her a bag of salt and sent her away. She cried so at having to leave that the whole road was strewn with pearls that had come from her tears.

The King soon learned that indeed, she loved him most of all. Only now, we do not know where she may be. We have searched and searched and have found no sign of her. Until today, when you have shown us this pearl, exactly the kind as those that used to fall from my daughter's eyes." The young gentleman then pledged that he would take the King and Queen to the old woman's hut in the forest. They set off at once.

The old woman and her ugly daughter were sitting in their hut until it became quite dark, the only light coming from the light of the full moon. The old woman looked up, "Now, my little daughter, it is time for you to go do your work." The daughter then left the hut to go through a meadow and into a valley. At last she came to a well with three large trees standing beside it.

The daughter removed a skin which covered her face and bent down into the well to wash herself. When she was finished, the maiden was changed. Her golden hair was like sunshine and her eyes shone like the stars. But the fair maiden was sad. She knelt down and wept bitterly. As the tears came out of her eyes, they formed jewels and pearls. She sat for a long time until she heard a rustling and cracking. She sprang up and put on the old skin and in an instant was gone, running back home.

When she returned, the old woman asked, "Do you remember what day it is today?"

"It is three years since I first came to you," replied the maiden.

"Yes. And now the time is up. We can no longer remain together."

"But dear mother, will you cast me out? I have no home, no friends to go to. I have always done what you have asked. Please do not send me away."

"My stay here is over," said the old woman kindly, "but when I leave the house must be clean. You shall have your wages, and a roof to shelter you. Have no care for yourself. Go to your chamber, remove the skin from your face and put on the gown you were wearing when you came to me." The girl then did as she was told.

The King and Queen had traveled with the young gentleman. He had left the King and Queen in a clearing that night, searching the valley for any sign of the old woman. He had been by the well when the ugly daughter had come to wash. "Oho," he thought, "If she is here, the old woman cannot be far." But how astonished he was when she went to the well and removed the skin. She was more beautiful than anyone he had ever seen. In trying to see her more clearly, he rustled through the trees. That noise had startled the girl and she had run off.

The young gentleman ran to the King and Queen and together they started in the direction that the beautiful girl had gone. Soon they were able to see the light shining out of the old woman's hut. The geese were sitting around it, sleeping. They peeked through the window and saw the old woman spinning in a perfectly clean room. The girl was nowhere to be seen.

They knocked on the door, and the old woman answered it, seemingly expecting them. "Come in, I know you already." When they had all entered the room, the old woman said, "You might have spared yourself the long walk if you had not unjustly sent your daughter away. No harm has come to the kind child. She is good. You have been sufficiently punished for the misery you have inflicted." She then called for the girl.

The princess then stepped into the room, and fell upon her father and mother. They all wept for joy. "My daughter," the King said, "your sisters have each been promised half of my kingdom. What can I give you?"

"She needs nothing," replied the old woman. "Her wages are the tears that she has wept on your account. They are finer jewels and pearls than any in your kingdom. I also give her my little house as payment for her services." The old woman smiled and then disappeared from their sight. The King, Queen, Princess, and gentleman looked around at the little hut that had changed into a palace.

The gentleman and the Princess married and remained together in the palace, happily ever after.

German Food

Germans are famous for their beautiful cakes and pastries. This cake, Schwarzwälder Kirschtorte or Black Forest Cherry Cake is named after the Black Forest in Southwestern Germany

Black Forest Cherry Cake-- 16 servings

CAKE
6 oz semisweet chocolate
3/4 cup butter
3/4 cup sugar
6 eggs

3/4 cup ground almonds
1 1/4 cup flour
1 1/2 teaspoon baking powder

FILLING AND TOPPING
3 envelopes unflavored gelatin
1/3 cup hot water
3 cups whipping cream
3/4 cup powdered sugar
2 cans pitted dark sweet cherries.
16 marachino cherries
2 Chocolate bars at room temperature

To make the cake, microwave chocolate until melted in a microwave safe bowl. Cream butter and sugar and add eggs, almonds and chocolate. Mix until light and fluffy. Fold in flour and baking powder. Bake in three greased round pans for 20 to 25 minutes at 350° and cool thoroughly.

Drain cherries. Dissolve gelatin in water and cool slightly. Whip cream with powdered sugar until stiff. Add cooled gelatin and mix well. Spread one layer of the cake with 1/4 of the whipping cream and arrange half of the canned cherries on the cream. Add second layer and top with more whipping cream and the rest of the canned cherries. Add third layer and spread tops and sides of cake with whipping cream. Pipe 16 rosettes of cream around the top of the cake and top each rosette with a maraschino cherry. Scrape chocolate bars with a vegetable peeler to create chocolate curls and pile on top of the cake. Sprinkle broken pieces of chocolate on the sides of the cake.

Color the Flag

1. Color all of the #1 area black
2. Color all of the #2 area red
3. Color all of the #3 area gold

The German flag is nicknamed the "Schwarz—Rot—Gold" ("black, red and gold") These are also the three colors of Germany's coat of arms. The colors symbolize German freedom and democracy. This flag has now represented German unity off and on since the 1800s. Each German state also has its own flag.

A Letter to My Ancestor

What would you say to your ancestor if you could talk to them today?

Dear _____

Sincerely,

_____

Oh Yeah? Prove It.

Documents prove what happened in the past. What documents have come from your German family's life that will prove to someone in the future that they were alive?

Paste an envelope here.
Make copies of documents from your ancestor's life, like
letters, civil registration, census, church and probate records and pictures.
Store your own copies of these documents in this envelope.
Original copies of important items should be kept in a very safe place.

German Music

Our German ancestors enjoyed a rich heritage of beautiful music. Many of the world's greatest composers were German. Johann Sebastian Bach, Ludwig van Beethoven and Johannes Brahms are just a few of the many great German music masters.

Commonly known as Für Elise, Bagatelle No. 25 in A Minor is one of Ludwig van Beethoven's most popular compositions. Beethoven died in 1827, and the song was not published until 1867, but according to some musicologists was originally written in 1810. In about 1800 Beethoven began to lose his hearing and he was completely deaf for the last 10 years of his life. With the popularity of the song, it is likely that many of your ancestors heard it.

Für Elise (Bagatelle No. 25 in A Minor)

Ludwig Van Beethoven

"Wiegenlied: Guten Abend, Gute Nacht", Op. 49, No. 4, was published by Johannes Brahms in 1868. The lyrics originally are from a collection of German folk poems. The song is now one of the most recognized melodies in the world.

Brahms Lullaby (Op.49 No. 4)

Johannes Brahms

Original German Lyrics

Guten Abend, gute Nacht,
mit Rosen bedacht,
mit Näglein besteckt,
schlupf' unter die Deck!
Morgen früh, wenn Gott will,
wirst du wieder geweckt.

Guten Abend, gute Nacht,
von Englein bewacht,
die zeigen im Traum
dir Christkindleins Baum.
Schlaf nun selig und süß,
schau im Traum's Paradies.

Literal English translation

Good evening, good night,
With roses covered,
With carnations adorned,
Slip under the covers.
Tomorrow morning, if God wants so,
you will wake once again.

Good evening, good night.
By angels watched,
Who show you in your dream
the Christ-child's tree.
Sleep now blissfully and sweetly,
see the paradise in your dream.

Traditional English version

Lullaby and good night,
With roses bedight,
With lilies o'er spread
Is baby's wee bed.
Lay thee down now and rest,
May thy slumber be blessed.

Lullaby and good night,
Thy mother's delight,
Bright angels beside
My darling abide.
They will guard thee at rest,
Thou shalt wake on my breast.

Weihnachten Activities

Germans have loved Christmas (Weihnachten) for hundreds of years. Preparations start on the first Sunday of Advent with activities leading up to the great event. Many American Christmas traditions come from Germany with one difference. In Germany children receive presents twice at Christmastime!

Advent

Advent marked the start of the Christmas season in German tradition. Every Sunday for four weeks before Christmas, families lit candles placed in an advent wreath. Families read scriptures, sung Christmas carols and ate Christmas treats while the candles burned.

Family History Advent Calendar Project

On a large piece of thin cardboard or posterboard, draw a Christmas picture with colored pencils or markers. Arrange 24 squares around the picture and number them 1 to 24. Cut three sides of each square to make a small door. Print small surprises for the inside of each of the boxes. You could use ancestor pictures, family traditions to be observed each day, or parts of a family Christmas story. Trim each surprise leaving 1/4 to 1/2 margins around each picture. Carefully glue the pictures behind each door making sure the doors still open. If you use ancestor pictures for the surprises, on the inside of each door, write the name and birthdates for each person in the picture. Starting on December 1st, open one door each day and have an older family member tell you a story about each day's ancestor or tradition.

In the early 1800s, Lutheran families began counting down the days of December until Christmas came. At first, the family would draw a chalk line on the door each day. Towards the end of the 1800s, people started creating Advent Calendars (Adventskalender) which were a fun way to get excited about Christmas. A calendar was usually made of cardboard and had 24 doors to open for each day leading up to Christmas. Older Advent calendars had pictures, or a part of a poem or story behind each opening but modern Advent calendars can be purchased with candy or small toys.

Make this Christbaumornament with the instructions on the opposite page.

Christmas Market (Weihnachtsmärkt)

Nearly 300 years ago, Germans began their Christmas celebrations by going to the Weihnachtsmärkt. When Advent started, Christmas Markets appeared in the town square of every German town. Our ancestors bought everything they needed for their Christmas celebration in the open air stalls at the market, Christmas decorations, candles, toys and all sorts of good things to eat and drink. The markets stayed open after dark when they twinkled with lights and the air filled with the smell of Christmas goodies.

To assemble the Christbaumornament for your Christmas tree:
Copy this page cut out the star. Color the outside star and carefully cut out the inside of the star. Cut along the dotted lines to create two tabs. Fold tab one forward, and fold tab two backward. Fit the platform into the star and glue tabs 1 and 2 onto the bottom of the platform. Color and cut out the manger and fold tab A to the back and tab B to the front. Glue tab A and B down to the Platform. String a ribbon through the hole at the top and hang the ornament.
You can make more ornaments substituting other pictures, or even pictures of your ancestors for the manger.

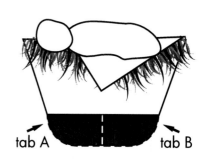

tab A   tab B

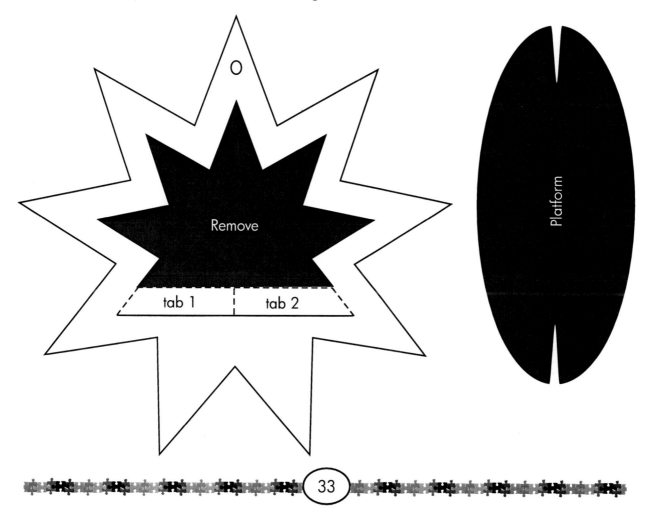

Weihnachtsmärkt continued

One of the treats at the Christmas Market was always Gingerbread (Lebkuchen) cut into festive shapes and decorated with nuts and candies and icing. Gingerbread houses became popular with the "Hansel and Gretel" folktale and children enjoyed making and decorating houses with their families.

Decorate the Lebkuchenhaus below. Then ask an adult to make one with you using the recipes on the next page.

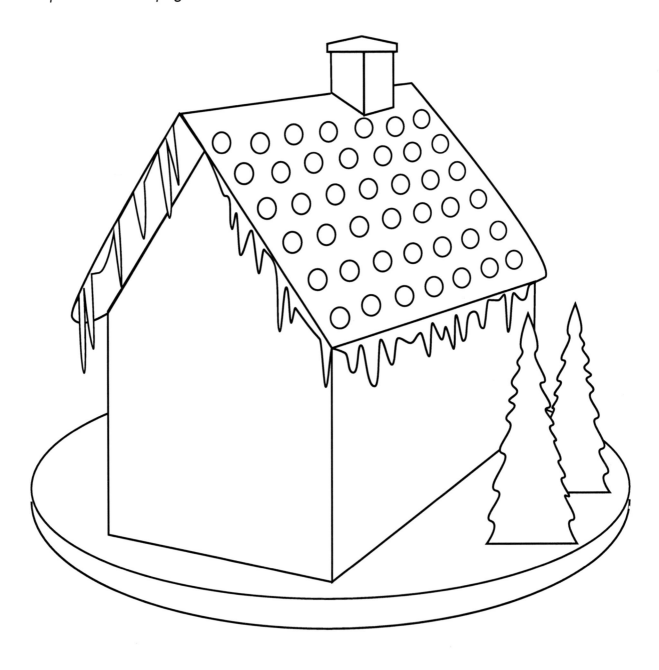

Gingerbread House (Lebkuchenhaus)

1/2 cup brown sugar
1/2 cup molasses
1/2 cup butter
Cream together then add:

1 teaspoon each, cloves, allspice, cinnamon and ginger
1 teaspoon baking soda
2 cups flour
2 tablespoons water
Combine to make thick dough. Refrigerate 1 hour before cutting out shapes.

Make a gingerbread house model of a home in your family's history. Construct a pattern for the gingerbread house out of cardstock paper and tape together to make sure the pieces will fit together right. Roll the dough 1/4 to 1/8 inch thick and cut out pieces for the gingerbread house. Bake at 375° for 15 minutes until firm. Trim the edges of the cookie pieces while warm and let cool. Assemble and decorate with royal icing, nuts and candies.

Royal Icing for Gingerbread Houses

3 cups powdered sugar
1/4 teaspoon cream of tartar
2 egg whites or 5 tablespoons meringue powder
1/4 teaspoon lemon juice

Mix the dry ingredients together. Using an electric mixer, beat the egg whites until stiff, and then combine into the dry mixture. Beat for about 5 minutes or until the mixture is thick enough to hold its shape. Royal Icing dries hard—perfect to hold gingerbread houses together.

St. Nicholas Day and St. Martin's Day

In Northern Germany, on the night of December 5th, German children cleaned their shoes and put them outside their doors hoping that St. Nicholas would come. During the night, St. Nikolaus came to visit, and he brought a book which had all of the names of bad children written in it. If the child had behaved well, their shoes would be filled with candies, cookies and fruit. But if they had not, they received nothing but a stick in their shoes. St. Nikolaus Day (Sankt Nikolaus Tag) celebrated Saint Nicholas who was a bishop in the Catholic Church that lived in the 4th century. Legend says he was famous for his kindness to children.

In Southern Germany many people celebrated St. Martin's Day (Martinmas) on November 11th instead of St. Nicholas Day. Children made paper lanterns in school and held a parade from the church to the main city square. A large bonfire was lit in the square to celebrate the light that St. Martin brought to poor people through his good deeds. Families feast on St. Martin's goose (Martinsgans). Children in the south would also receive candy if they were good and coal if they were not on St. Martin's Day.

Christmas Eve and Christmas Day

Christmas Eve (Heiliger Abend) was an important celebration for German families. In Northern areas of Germany, the Christmas Man (Weihnachtsmann) brought more gifts on Christmas Eve and in Southern areas a messenger from Baby Jesus (Christkind) brought the gifts. The main Christmas celebrations took place on Christmas Eve rather than Christmas Day. Gifts were opened and families had dinner and went to a church service together. A special midnight Christmas service was given in church. On Christmas Day (Weihnachts Tag) extended families visited and more feasts of traditional goose with red cabbage and dumplings were shared.

Red Cabbage (Rotkohl)
1 large firm head of red cabbage chopped
2 apples peeled and diced
1 teaspoon salt
3 Tablespoons sugar
1 teaspoon caraway seeds
2 tablespoons shortening
1 tablespoon lemon juice or vinegar

Cover cabbage and apples with boiling water. Add salt, sugar, shortening and lemon juice or vinegar and cook on low heat on the stove for two hours.

Christmas Tree (Tannenbaum)

Germans have been decorating Christmas trees (Tannenbäume) since the 1400s with tinsel, glass balls and sweets. Real candles were used to decorate instead of electric lights. Parents would decorate the tree on Christmas Eve (Heiliger Abend) behind closed doors and excited children were allowed to see the tree and join the festivities once the candles were lit. Evergreen trees, holly and other plants which keep their green color in the winter were brought indoors to brighten the dreary winter months. Germans immigrants brought the Christmas tree custom with them to America and spread the tradition throughout the world.

Today, electric Christmas lights are much safer than candles on a Christmas tree. But you can still honor your ancestors with candles on your Christmas tree that you make yourself. Create a family history Christmas tree by displaying small pictures of your ancestors and other ornaments that represent their lives.

Make a Christmas tree candle by copying this page and cutting out the pieces. Roll the candle into a tube and glue together. Fold the tabs inside and glue them to the base. Glue the loop into a circle and attach it to the bottom of the base so that you can fasten it around the tree branches. Cut 1 inch squares of red and orange and yellow tissue paper. Poke a couple of pieces of tissue together in the top of the candle to create a flame.

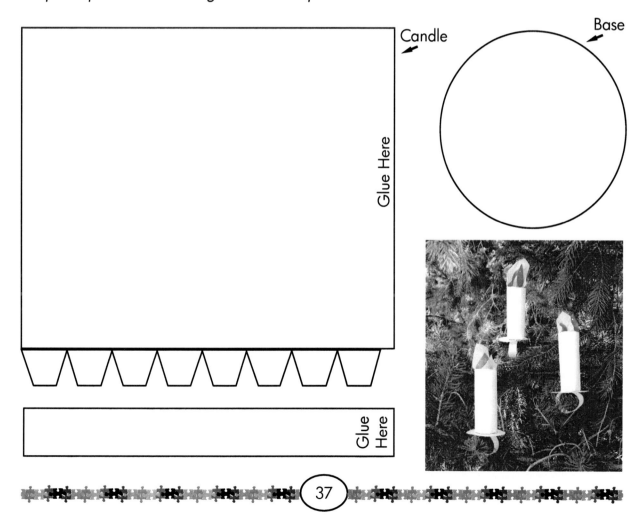

Candle

Base

Glue Here

Glue Here

Gothic German Script

German is a very old language. German documents as old as 800 AD were written in German Gothic Script which can be like a secret code when you are trying to find out more about your German ancestors. Some of your ancestor's documents may be written in Gothic script. When you are reading them you have to be very careful to pay attention to the details because many letters are very similar and sometimes it is hard to tell where one letter ends and another starts. Try your hand at Gothic German script here.

A	B	C	D
E	F	G	H
I	J	K	L
M	N	O	P
Q	R	S	T
U	V	W	X
Y	Z		

Write your ancestor's name here in Gothic Script:

Practice writing secret messages to your family members in Gothic Script and you will soon be able to read your ancestors' documents easily.

Paper Dolls

Color and cut out these paper dolls. You can play with them and use them to tell your family members stories about your ancestors.

Paper Doll Clothes

Modern and superhero clothing can be downloaded at www.zapthegrandmagap.com

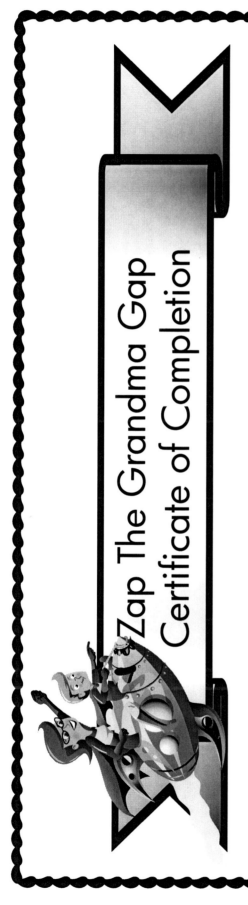

Zap The Grandma Gap
Certificate of Completion

_____

has been able to bridge the gap and learn about

_____

their German ancestor.

Thanks to _____

for helping complete the activities and research in this workbook.

_____
Date

Answers

Do You Know German?

Complete the puzzle to learn some words your German ancestors used.

German sometimes uses diacritical marks with their letters such as:
ä (which usually makes the sound eh as in ted)
ö (which usually makes the sound i as in girl)
ü (which usually makes the sound oo like in mood)
ß (which usually makes the sound ss)
Some of these letters may be found in this puzzle.

Across
2. brothers
4. married
7. ancestors
8. daughters
9. brother-in-law
12. Mom
13. grandmother

Down
1. family
3. parents
5. siblings
6. uncle
7. father
10. family tree
11. cousin

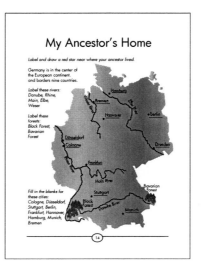

My Ancestor's Home

Label and draw a red star near where your ancestor lived.

Germany is in the center of the European continent. and borders nine countries.

Label these rivers:
Danube, Rhine, Main, Elbe, Weser

Label these forests:
Black Forest, Bavarian Forest

Fill in the blanks for these cities:
Cologne, Düsseldorf, Stuttgart, Berlin, Frankfurt, Hannover, Hamburg, Munich, Bremen

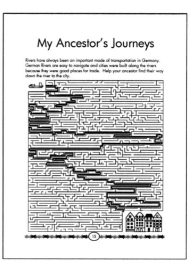

My Ancestor's Journeys

Rivers have always been an important mode of transportation in Germany. German Rivers are easy to navigate and cities were built along the rivers because they were good places for trade. Help your ancestor find their way down the river to the city.

German Länder

German borders have changed many times during many wars. Throughout much of history, small Germanic Länder (states) were ruled by dynasties (families) of princes, dukes, and kings. If your ancestor lived in the German Empire (1871-1918), their hometown may now be in Belgium, Czech Republic, Denmark, France, Lithuania,

Unscramble the names of some of the historic kingdoms in the German Empire (1871-1918) and solve the puzzle to find the name of Germany's first Chancellor.

The first chancellor of Germany was a Prussian diplomat who wanted to create a unified German nation. He was the leader of the largest and most powerful is Brandenburg-Prussia. For many years, he led his state into wars with neighboring states to bring them into one federation. Separate Germanic states unified in 1871 to make the German

LEIPP — LIPPE
LEKCBU — LUBECK
SIARUPS — PRUSSIA
LUBRONGED — OLDENBURG
WEIRUNSAHBCG — BRAUNSCHWEIG
SACLAE RRALNIEO — ALSACE LORRAINE

OTTO VON BISMARCK

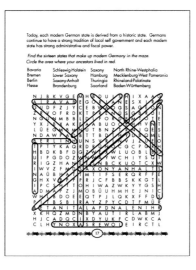

Today, each modern German state is derived from a historic state. Germans continue to have a strong tradition of local self government and each modern state has strong administrative and fiscal power.

Find the sixteen states that make up modern Germany in the maze. Circle the area where your ancestors lived in red.

Bavaria
Bremen
Berlin
Hesse

Schleswig-Holstein
Lower Saxony
Saxony-Anhalt
Brandenburg

Saxony
Hamburg
Thuringia
Saarland

North Rhine-Westphalia
Mecklenburg-West Pomerania
Rhineland-Palatinate
Baden-Württemberg

German Innovators

Germans have made many innovations that changed the world of our ancestors. Until the early 1400s every book had to be copied by hand. But around 1440, Johannes Gutenberg invented the printing press which could print dozens of pages a day. The most important book Gutenberg printed was the Bible. For the first time, many people could read the Bible themselves instead of just listening to Bible stories in church.

Gutenberg's Bible made it possible for another German innovator to spark a religious reformation and start a new religion. In 1517 Martin Luther, a German priest, nailed a list of 95 scholarly challenges called "theses" to the door of the church. Many people agreed with him and eventually the new Lutheran church was formed. Other Protestant churches were also formed as people protested against the dominant church.

Gutenberg's press used movable type—letters that could be re-arranged to make different pages and different books. The letters from Gutenberg's press have fallen on the floor. Can you help him put each letter back in the proper place so that he can print the Gutenberg Bible?

BUT I WILL FOR THEIR SAKES REMEMBER THE COVENANT OF THEIR ANCESTORS. LEVITICUS 26:45

Further Resources

See also the Genealogy Resources on page 8.

For more information about German culture and history:

germanhistorydocs.ghi-dc.org
   A beautiful site with primary source materials about German history.
www.germanculture.com.ua
   Lots of information about the history, language, traditions and culture of
   Germany.
www.goethe.de
   Click on the British flag in the top right corner to change the website to
   English. The official organization for the promotion of all things German.
www.germany-info.org.
   The official website of the German embassy in the United States.
www.tatsachen-ueber-deutschland.de/en
   A reference site full of articles about modern and historical Germany.
timeforkids.com/destination/germany
   A great timeline, audio of how to pronounce German words and a day in
   the life of what one of your German cousins may be doing now.

Parnell, Helga. *Cooking the German Way.* Minneapolis: Lerner Publications
   Company, 2003.
Foley, Ronan. *A River Journey: The Rhine.* Chicago: Raintree, 2004.
Russell, Henry. *Countries of the World: Germany.* National Geographic
   Society: Washington, 2007.
Davis, Kevin A. *Look What Came From Germany.* Franklin Watts: London,
   2000.

Take a look at **zapthegrandmagap.com** for more ideas and free down-
loads to explore your family history and make it fun for all ages:
   •Get the book *Zap The Grandma Gap: Connect to Your Family By
    Connecting The To Their Family History* and it's companion *Power Up
    Workbook* for 100s of easy family history ideas.
   •Sign up on the website for the weekly newsletter with one simple idea
    each week to create stronger bonds in your family.